#163

"Back 9 Walking:

A Guide to Living Life Unleashed"

Dan Weedin

Back 9 Walking – A Guide to Living Life Unleashed

First published in 2021 by
Dan Weedin
Poulsbo, WA, USA

ISBN: 9798785447561 (paperback)
ISBN: 9798786013659 (hard cover)

Business

Editing: Linda Popky, Leverage2Market Associates, Inc (USA)
www.leverage2market.com

Cover Design: Shiloh Schroeder, Fusion Creative Works (USA)
www.fusioncw.com

Interior Design/Self-Publishing: Lyn Prowse-Bishop, Executive Stress Office Support (Australia) www.execstress.com

Table of Contents

Introduction: Making the Turn

My ball. My destiny.

This book isn't about golf. It's not about dogs. Yet both are a major part of how you will read my ideas and concepts about walking the Back Nine of life unleashed.

One of the things I love about the game of golf is that my results are solely dependent on me. I'm not being defended against, as in basketball. There's no one returning my serve, as in tennis. There are no foes trying to tackle me, as in football, or to pitch a ball I'm supposed to try and hit, as in baseball.

It's just me against me with my own golf ball. I may battle adverse weather conditions. I will certainly be tested by the terrain. Yet, ultimately, golf will expose my skills and decisions—whether they be good or bad, for me and my playing partners to see—for that day.

And then we do it again.

Sounds like life.

Over the past year, my faithful canine companion has slowed down. Captain Jack is about 14 ½ years old as I write this book.

He used to be an exuberant walker from porch step back to the front door. Recently, something has happened on the first part of our mile-long walk.

If you were an observer, you'd be certain I was kidnapping a dog. I'm literally dragging Captain Jack by his leash with both hands. He's got a dual leash on (due to his past escapes and escapades)—one linked to his harness, and the other at his collar. Jack wants to go anywhere but forward. He's slow, deliberate, turning back, turning sideways, grunting his displeasure. He and I both need the exercise, so we march on ...

And then we hit *the turn.*

In golf, the turn signifies the halfway point of an 18-hole round. On older courses, you head *out* on the course, make the turn, and head back *in to* the clubhouse. Now many courses have you making the turn back at the clubhouse, probably so you can buy more food and beverages!

At the turn, you transition from the *Front Nine* to the *Back Nine.*

For Captain Jack, the turn is at the park. At that magical spot, he changes back into the dynamo of old and we are on a hot-footed walk all the way home. I started telling him that while he was a terrible Front Nine walker, he brought his A-game to the Back Nine. That's a plus, as we all want to finish strong, right?

Which got me thinking.

Captain Jack and I are both on the Back Nine of life. In my mid-50s, even if I hit my goal of the century mark, I've definitely made the turn. Am I as prepared to be a dynamo on my own Back Nine walk?

For those of us over 40 years old, we should by now understand that things change a lot—physically, mentally, and emotionally. Relationships with family and friends will shift. And our priorities and perspectives will change. Our parents will transition to a later part of their own journeys (often painfully for adult children), while our children will start fearlessly playing their own Front Nine. Resilience takes on a whole new meaning on The Back Nine.

A recent global pandemic made us all stop in our tracks and assess our own mortality and quality of life and lifestyle.

I've worked with countless business owners and leaders over a 30+ year career. I know with certainty that how each of us deals with relationships, adversity, mindset, priorities, and worldview will expose our "game" to us, and to those with whom we choose to play.

Through my own experiences, expertise, and observations, I've identified some things that have become important to me as I try to mirror Captain Jack's Back Nine exuberance. As a bonus, Captain Jack has nicely agreed to share his insights throughout the book, as well.

My hope is that this book will give you ideas on how to best play your own Back Nine, regardless of where you are on that path. Just like on a golf course, you can start at the beginning, or play through and begin at any chapter you want. If you're still on the Front Nine, even better. You may end up with a new perspective of what's in store for you.

I wouldn't change a thing from my Front Nine, including the triple-bogeys that littered a few of the holes. The reason? Because I believe in The Butterfly Effect—or as I like to call it, The Marty McFly Effect (from the movie, *Back to the Future*)[1]. Any change in the past would have changed where I am today, and altered the people and relationships that are part of my life.

Now my focus is the same as in golf: Learn from the previous holes to assure that the rest of the round is the most fun, rewarding, and unleashed. Because in life, we only get this one round.

Thanks for coming along for the walk ...

---

[1] *"Back to the Future,"* IMDb, https://www.imdb.com/title/tt0088763/.

A Word about the Front Nine...

You may be wondering why this book starts with Hole 10 ... what about the Front Nine?

Here's the thing. On the Front Nine of a round of golf, there's always great anticipation. No matter how many times I've played a course, I'm excited for what's ahead. I'm confident, fearless, and jovial. Then we tee off on the first hole!

On the golf course, we start learning about how the course is playing, and, if it's new to us, we get a feel for what kind of course it will be. Along the way, we get a whole bunch of experiences, both good and bad. From those experiences, our initial feelings of confidence and fearlessness will also change and develop.

Then we make the turn at the 10th hole.

At least for me, my first 40 or so years of life very much mirrored a Front Nine on the course. I was self-assured and found myself being a regular risk-taker. In golf, it's the equivalent of going after every pin, regardless of the danger. As my own personal Front Nine evolved, new obstacles would kick me in the teeth occasionally, but I could easily get off the mat and move forward—although never without the experience leaving a mark and sometimes even a scar.

As I became a father and became responsible for not just myself but for the well-being of others, I had more reasons to be more careful. Along the way, jobs, career, and opportunities for growth presented themselves. As the time came to make my own turn in life, those experiences and education forced me to have a new perspective on my Back Nine—as it does for all of us.

And that's what I want to share with you in this book.

Dan Weedin
December 2021

The 10th Hole: Identity

The Drive: Where did you come from?

"My middle name is Joseph."

Actually, it's not.

My real middle name is José. I was named after my maternal grandfather José Antonio González. Tonito, as he was fondly called by his grandchildren in Colombia, lived with my family for ten years after the death of his wife, my grandmother.

From the time I was 2 until I turned 12, when he returned to play out his "final rounds" in his beloved Bogotá, Tonito was a presence in my life and home. While I was in my formative years, Tonito was in his 80s and ultimately lived to the ripe "young" age of 96.

When I was in 1st Grade, I was asked by my teacher, Miss Lawrence, to reveal my middle name. The reason? There were two boys named "Danny" in the class. My name at home was always Danny, and that continued throughout my life with my family and friends. Miss Lawrence's attempt to find a solution to the potential confusion was laudable and made sense.

I correctly replied that, "My middle name is José."

After a brief pause, I heard giggling. It was the type of giggling that starts small with 6-year-olds and then soon after turns to laughter. As my face started to feel flushed, Miss Lawrence gently intervened to quell the laughter. I quickly turned the tide by telling her that I was fine with being called "Dan." And that was that.

Miss Lawrence thought my middle name was cool: my classmates thought it was comical.

Now don't misunderstand—I didn't feel picked on or bullied. In fact, had I been in their position, I might have been inclined to join along with the guffaws. That's a common trait in groups where acceptance is coveted and valued over everything else.

At 6 years old, I was bilingual. I'd spent the summer of 1971 in Bogotá visiting family with Mom and Tonito. Upon coming home, my Spanish skills eventually faded.

Even though Tonito lived with us for a decade during my developmental years, Spanish wasn't spoken in our house. He didn't speak a word of English, although I think he secretly knew more than he let on. He uncannily always found ways to communicate well through his charm, guile, and personality.

Dad didn't speak Spanish and had no desire to do so. After almost a decade of living in the Unites States, Mom had transitioned into being the "American wife," and acquiesced to becoming the interpreter.

In retrospect, my reluctance to embrace the Spanish language that was such an important part of my heritage has become one of the very few regrets of my life. To be clear, I don't hold either of my parents culpable. This was just how it was in the 1970s, which was the problem.

Furthermore, at a young age, I found myself being embarrassed by Mom's Spanish accent. I was indifferent to the fact that she was completely fluent in two languages—my childhood fear was being considered "different" than others.

In my naturally teenage selfish fashion, I didn't consider Mom's accent and the amusement at my expense at school to be something that should be continued. It was a situation I could control. At the next opportunity to respond to the question of my middle name (which surprisingly came up a lot in grade school), I cavalierly deserted my family ancestry for the Americanized version of the name—Joseph.

Fast forward about fifteen years to 1986.

My then fiancée, Barb, and I were months away from being married. She excitedly revealed a surprise to me one afternoon: The wedding invitations had arrived.

Earlier in the preparations, I had gladly ceded all design and verbiage to Barb and her mother. I was fully prepared to show as much enthusiasm toward these announcements as I deemed appropriate.

She opened the box and enthusiastically showed me the announcement. To my great horror (and anguish), I slowly read the name of the groom—*Daniel Joseph Weedin*.

The sound of silence in my brain was deafening.

I'm sure Barb thought my momentary gasp to begin breathing again was one of pure delight for the product. It wasn't.

My sudden realization was that this invitation was irreversible. My mother would see it and all of my family members in Colombia would also receive the invitation with the English version of my grandfather's name—just three years after his passing.

I had to confess, and fast.

Let me cut to and from the next scene quickly: Barb was furious. In fact, thirty-five years later, even after full repentance, the story draws an acerbic eye roll!

First, I'd been dishonest to her, even though it wasn't intentional. In reality, I'd embraced the fabrication to the point that I believed that Joseph was in fact my middle name!

Second, this invitation would be one of the lifetime keepsakes of what was to be a major life event. This was her creation, and the fact that her soon to be mother-in-law might hold her responsible for the inaccuracy was an embarrassment.

Of course, I was the one who had to break the news to Mom. I remember it as if it were yesterday. She graciously accepted the apology, though I could feel the hurt within her.

Even though I didn't realize it at the time, it was at that moment that my identity of who I was and where I came from began to be evident.

My desire to not be singled-out—to not be considered as different—was so strong that I was willing to abandon where I came from. It was born out of a bias that wasn't malicious, but very subtle.

This bias isn't intrinsic: it's observed and learned. In my case, this bias became so rooted that as mentioned earlier, I started *believing* that Joseph was my middle name until I got punched in my soul on that fateful afternoon.

I reiterate, this is NOT a condemnation of my parents or my schoolmates. While I'm personally ashamed about this, I don't rebuke myself too much. However, if I allow my observation of these events from over forty years ago to pass by without some reflection and attempt to improve, then I've missed an opportunity for growth and maturity.

I have now fully embraced my middle name. I'm proud to be named after my grandfather. In fact, my formal signature now includes the entire name, not just the initial.

I know from where I came, and I have the name to prove it.

What's Your Identity?

Over the past three decades of working with business owners, entrepreneurs, and professionals, I've encountered a common trait.

Like the bias mentioned in my story, this trait is very subtle. So subtle that if left to its own devices, it could become dangerous. That trait is identifying one's self with their business or work. More clearly, it's defining one's value as a person with the company they've founded or the work they do.

Founding and owning a company is personal. It's not just a *job*, rather it's a personal statement of who one is. Being a business owner or entrepreneur is a label that can easily be affixed to identity. With that label comes fear, trepidation, stress, courage, grit, passion, resilience, and determination, to name a few.

I didn't mention *humanity*. Unfortunately, just as I came to believe that Joseph was my middle name, too many business leaders judge their humanity on success, mediocrity, or failure in their company or vocation.

Hoop Dreams

Basketball has been a game I've played all my life and I'd come to love. I still remember Dad putting up the hoop in the driveway, and all the neighborhood kids coming to my house to shoot hoops and play pickup games.

I was good enough to play on school teams from 6th Grade through my junior year in high school. Through those years, being a basketball player had become part of my identity—even though I didn't realize it.

One of the challenges was that I realized I wasn't good enough to earn playing time as a senior. I was afraid of making the team and being relegated to the end of the bench. I wasn't willing to see myself as a valuable member of the team as a practice player and encourager; rather, I feared what others in the school would think of my identity as a basketball player.

To control my own identity once again, I told the head coach that I wasn't turning out for my senior year. I came to him offering to be the person who kept the score book for road games. In my mind, I was still somewhat a member of the team—without the concern of judgment.

Coach Nelson seemed a bit sad and asked if I was sure of this decision. Why not try out and see how things went? I assured him I was certain and would happily take my "talents" to the intramural court and help the team as I could. I'm guessing Coach Nelson knew the value of every player on the team, including seniors who could offer value even when not playing in games.

I had the privilege of coaching girls' high school basketball for six years. I was inspired by coaches like Coach Nelson and started coaching Little League when I was still in high school. When my daughters were old enough to start playing, I enthusiastically coached their teams with what I deemed to be great success—winning a lot of games.

Through a little bit of luck, I was hired by North Kitsap High School to coach the girls' team. I had actually been hoping to get the assistant job but must have interviewed well enough to get the top spot.

In my first year, we started fast. We won eight of our first ten games, and in my mind, this was the same as my "success" before. That year, we finished 10-10, and that would be my best season record.

Over those six years, I worked hard to be a better coach. I cared about my players as people. I wanted them to develop as players and humans, and I tried to put them in a position to be the best they could be. I also deeply wanted to win because I had fooled myself into thinking this was part of my identity.

Just as in high school, I was cognizant of the judgment of others. *Failure* as a coach meant losing seasons and no playoffs. That little voice that emanated from the back of my head kept telling me that my value as a person was tied to my record as a basketball coach.

While at the time I would eschew that theory, in truth I couldn't bring myself to even tell family and friends what my six-year record as a coach was for nearly ten years after I "retired" to start my consulting practice.

39-81. Thirty-nine wins versus eighty-one losses. That's a winning percentage of only 32.5%.

During that time and for a healthy period afterwards, my identity as a basketball coach was fixed to my record, and I allowed the judgement of myself as a person to be tied to that.

So, what about you?

We all hold fast to something that we consider part of our identity, don't we?

Business owners, executives, and entrepreneurs are susceptible to being defined and identified by their *success* in business. Each person will define success differently. It might mean revenue generation and growth, reputation based on who their clients are, number of employees, number of years in business, accolades of others, or awards and achievements bestowed.

It's not only business owners and entrepreneurs, either. Those of you who are in sales, advertising, product development, or leadership positions also are subject to identifying with your vocation.

In the end, the problem is a double-edged sword.

Too much success causes vanity, self-importance, and smugness. Often this leads to setting expectations that cause unintended pressure.

Too little success based on self-centered metrics can lead to anxiety, depression, and lack of self-esteem.

You've heard about the imposter syndrome?

The **imposter syndrome** is defined as "a psychological pattern in which an individual doubts their skills, talents, or accomplishments and has a persistent internalized fear of being exposed as a fraud."[2] Despite external evidence of their competence, those experiencing this phenomenon remain convinced that they are frauds and do not deserve all they have achieved.

This malady is not uncommon in CEOs and business owners. Those that experience it are good at hiding it well. I certainly can look back at my years as a coach and understand that I ended up feeling like an imposter—even though I'd accomplished something incredibly unique for a non-educator.

---

[2] "You're Not a Fraud. Here's How to Recognize and Overcome Imposter Syndrome," *Healthline* blog. https://www.healthline.com/health/mental-health/imposter-syndrome#vs-discrimination

The Practice Range:

What's your identity?

Honestly. Without saying what you think it should be. What do you *really* believe is your identity?

This question really becomes important as we are Back Nine Walking. For me, it has taken decades of experiences and perspective to understand mine.

Here's my identity: Husband. Father. Grandfather. Son. Brother. Friend.

That's it.

The other things I once might include are what I *do*: Entrepreneur. Author. Podcaster. Educator. Rotarian. Golfer. Home cook. Dog walker ...

My activities (including my career) and my associations are all relevant but not defining. If I do the ones I've identified well, that's good enough.

Your turn on the practice range now.

Identify who you are. This isn't a fast or easy process. Keep it simple and honest. Get help from those you trust. Write down the answers.

You might find that one or more of the identities are given too much value, or what you value most isn't given enough time and investment.

The Front Nine formed us. On the Back Nine, we must be clear about our identity, so we can get the most out of each step of the walk.

Captain Jack on the Green

I go for walks with Dan. He's always in a hurry. I like taking my time and smelling the spots where other dogs have peed. Then I pee on top of it. He says we are exercising. I don't care.

Sometimes I hear people ask him if I'm a Jack Russell. What kind of a question is that? Look at me!

Then they ask if I'm a purebred.

Who cares?! After all, if there is ANY Jack Russell in a dog, you're the best dog on the planet. I know other breeds will object to that, and they are entitled to a wrong opinion.

Look ... I know humans think and worry a lot about who they are. Not dogs. We are clear about it.

We are dogs. We love our owners and will protect and defend them and our territory. We bark. We sniff. We pee where and when we want. We don't worry about s**t.

If people were more like dogs, they'd be happier. We know who we are and where we're going, even if we're stuck on the leash.

Forget being like a goldfish with a ten second memory. Just be like a dog.

Even better, be like me.

Captain Jack out ...

We all deal with insecurities.

Many of the most celebrated entertainers in the world suffered with imposter syndrome. Regardless of their fame and fortune, they were tortured with the concept of "Why me?" that has often been the cause of so many confusing drug addictions and suicides.

We will all have moments of great certainty and confidence, but we will also experience times when we doubt our own abilities and ask, why me?

As I wrote this book, I've asked myself those questions. The voice comes from the recesses of the back of my brain. It's that insidious proverbial little voice asking these questions:

"Why would anyone read your book?"

"Why would anyone care what you have to say?"

"Why are you an expert?"

Yeah, I've heard you. I'm just choosing to tell you to F-off. I'm busy writing.

We have to be resilient when we get smacked around by the outside world. We have to be even stronger in the face of an even harsher critic ... that little voice.

When that voice comes calling in your head—and it will—respond like I just did. Be strong and confident in yourself and your abilities, skills, and smarts.

Because if you don't, nobody else will.

Why you?

Why not!

The 11th Hole: Hobbies

What Hobby?

In my weekly podcast, I ask our guests a fun, hopefully thought-provoking question, that should be easy to answer. I'm intrigued to hear just how quickly they respond OR how hard it is to find an answer.

If you had to start another business from a hobby, what's the hobby and why?

My colleague and Shrimp Tank Podcast co-host Phil Symchych is the person who came up with this clever question. When he shared it with me, I had an immediate response.

Golf is the hobby. The idea would be to set up a boutique studio that has a golf simulator for people to use—either as a member or as a guest to host parties. It would be along the lines of a boutique Top Golf facility. Plus, I'd be able to use it for myself and my family!

I love the question and I thought that all guests would be immediately able to choose a hobby. That hasn't been the case. While many do have a hobby that immediately comes to mind—everything from beekeeping to baking—many struggle with it. Too frequently I hear, "I don't have time for hobbies."

Is this you?

If so, it should concern you, as it should my guests who answered the way they did.

The Family Jewels

When I was a kid, Dad had an interesting hobby. Somewhere along the line, he became fascinated with stones and the opportunity to make jewelry. He began going to the beach where we lived in Oak Harbor, WA, to collect interesting stones.

Dad built a little studio in the garage. He bought the tools and equipment to create beautiful jewelry, ranging from brooches to pins to necklaces. He had no interest in selling them. He made them for my mother, grandmother, aunt, sisters, and other family. His passion was the process.

Dad was wired to be process oriented. He was introspective, thoughtful, and meticulous when it came to his craft. He also was not much of a conversationalist, especially while working. My personal gift of loquaciousness must come from the González side of my family.

Dad made jewelry for several years, and then at some point that I don't remember, he simply stopped.

Years later, after my grandmother passed away, Dad doled out some of her jewelry to Barb and the girls. I remember asking him why he stopped making jewelry. His response was curious.

He said, "Nobody seemed to be interested in it, so I just stopped." That wasn't good enough for me. I inquired as to what that meant. Dad continued, "I was always out there alone. You and your mother never showed an interest."

I reminded Dad that I had been 13 years old. The only things that interested me at the time were sports and girls!

After Grandma died, Dad found a new hobby. Perhaps it might be better termed an obsession.

Dad went all-in on genealogy. He was fastidious in his research. This affinity began about 1998, so the Internet was not the tool it would later become. There was no Ancestry.com or DNA testing. It was the methodology of investigation and research that Dad loved.

I was busy being a father to teenagers, coaching them in sports, and building a career. I didn't have time for more than a casual interest. My mother had zero interest, although she was supportive (except for when it meant traipsing around gravesites looking for headstones—she drew the line there!).

Dad never relinquished his passion for genealogy. It was with him until he died, about thirteen years after he started his quest to find the family "jewels".

It has led me to wonder what the similarities and differences in these hobbies were. The main connection was the process—the method (maybe even the madness). Both jewelry making and genealogy required deep thinking, rather than being physical. They involved research and scrutiny, there were no time limits to the process, and an almost zealous demand for exactness.

Why did Dad leave jewelry making and not genealogy?

His stated reason was that he was making the jewelry by himself, and that no one showed an interest. Well, his work around genealogy was most often solo, and while the family all thought what he was doing was interesting, there was probably more affinity towards the jewelry!

I've concluded that Dad really had no skin in the game with the jewelry. It was simply the process he loved. It was an activity that got him away from his chair and the daily grind of a physical job. He was able to use his hands and create something that his wife, mother, and sister could wear. He wasn't someone who wore jewelry, so eventually the love of the process gave way to boredom.

Genealogy had meaning to him. Dad was deeply devoted to family. His curiosity for his own identity was rooted in his family tree, and it married perfectly with his insatiable desire to do research. Add to it that as he was now retired, he had all the time in the world to immerse himself.

To that end, I am confident that this passion added years to his life, and for that I'm incredibly grateful.

So, what about you?
We all had hobbies as kids.

For me, it was mostly around playing and watching sports—especially basketball, golf, football, and baseball. I collected sports cards and memorabilia.

After high school, I became enamored with lifting weights. In high school, it was more of a requirement for varsity conditioning. However, those of us playing basketball and especially golf were warned against getting too muscle-bound. Turns out that information was wrong.

Today, I've still got a few of those hobbies, specifically golf and fitness. They both look different, but I make them a priority because I love the physicality and rewards they each bring. And I've picked up a hobby I would never have imagined even fifteen years ago ... cooking. Barb is still amazed. She probably thought that my pastime of simply eating the food she cooked was going to be it for my life!

I love cooking. It's still physical (do you see a trend?) and there's a reward and satisfaction at the end.

For me, my hobbies are about physicality, rewards, and the endless striving to continue to improve the activity.

What's your hobby and why do you have it?

I think it's important to understand what drives you to garden, bake, keep bees, sew, play video games, play music, or whatever you choose for an avocation.

The reason? If you understand the why, you are more likely to continue and avoid boredom. You will find new ways to keep the joy fresh and build a strong relationship with your hobby.

There was a dark period in my golf game, when my skills deteriorated from lack of play. I then played less, because my results were dreadful, which just made things worse. My relationship with golf had deteriorated and I realized that in this case, it was me—not golf. I changed the relationship by making a commitment, setting new expectations, and making a new promise to myself to enjoy the moment.

Whatever your hobby, make your own commitment to keeping that relationship strong.

Like any healthy personal relationship, it will have high and low periods. By understanding the why, you will be the one in charge of keeping the relationship fresh!

Now for those of you who claim to be "hobby-less".

I hear statements like, "I don't have time for a hobby," or "My work is my hobby," and "I will get a hobby when I have more time..."

Blah, blah, blah.

Look, if you want to perform better in your career and be a more productive person, then hobbies are a necessary priority. They aid in de-stressing—which allows you to remain mentally sharp and productive. They drive innovation and creativity. Hobbies promote better physical and mental health—including reducing the risk of ailments like high blood pressure, heart disease, and depression.

In my own research, I've learned that creating a healthy balance in life with hobbies will also reduce the risk of many of the challenges of aging—including dementia and physical deterioration.

If you really want to be good at life—in both a personal and professional realm—as you walk the "fairways" of the Back Nine, then hobbies must be a ubiquitarian instrument in your bag.

The Practice Range:

Now it's time to get down to it ...

Take a few minutes to identify your hobbies. How long have you had them? Why do you like them? Do they provide joy and reward? Or do you have a potential "relationship problem" to fix?

If you aren't making time for a hobby at this stage of your life, you're making a mistake.

Why?

Because now, more than ever, we need to be re-charged, rejuvenated, and refreshed. The diversion of going to the driving range (or even outside with plastic golf balls) does wonders for me.

I have a client who loves video games. Great. If that's your passion, go play video games and become absorbed in them. What's your pleasure—gardening, cooking, making beer or wine, dancing, playing music, etc?

All hobbies bring value, because you focus on the task at hand and become mentally better when you come out the other end.

P.S. Your family isn't a hobby. Your family deserves better than that.

While you can find some things to do together, your hobby should be an activity that relaxes, de-stresses, and revitalizes you. Make a time commitment to your family (more on this on a later hole), and to your hobbies. Combine them when you can, but allow yourself to selfishly indulge in something from which you draw energy.

Captain Jack on the Green

I have a hobby.

I'm a snake hunter. And I'm good at it.

Those rascals like to hang out in the green bushes next to Sapna and Alex's house. They think that I'm too old and slow, but that plays to my advantage.

There are two keys to being a snake hunter. One is patience and the other is speed.

Patience is important because I must wait until the snake is positioned at an angle that allows me to grab it. You can tell when they're comfortable—little do they know.

Once the time is right, speed is everything. I take the straight-line attack leading with the nose. I know I only get one chance, so I make it a good one!

After catching a snake, the next thing to do is shake the pee out of it. We dogs are good at that. Dan then shakes me. He must think it's a game, but it works against me and sometimes I drop the snake. But the game is all about the catch.

This is my hobby. I love doing it, but if I was paid for it, I think I would lose the joy. You know how it is.

Captain Jack out …

The 12th Hole: Family

The Past

"I'm losing my mind, aren't I?"

These words were spoken by my mother as we sat at the dining room table one day playing Chinese Checkers.

"No, Mom. Why would you say that?"

"Because there are things I'm forgetting that I shouldn't forget and there are things that I should know that I don't."

Her voice trailed off and her eyes were looking in the distance. She knew exactly what she was asking. It broke my heart.

Of course, I lied to her. Mom was living with us now that Dad had passed away. She had frontal lobe dementia—a horrid and cruel disease. This was one of the last truly lucid moments for her. She knew, and I could feel the agony.

Alicia González was a vibrant personality in her youth. Growing up in a well-to-do family in Bogotá, Colombia, she went to work for my entrepreneur grandfather, who owned a men's fine clothing store in the city. She worked as a buyer, became bilingual, and frequently took buying trips to her favorite destination, New York City.

Later, in the mid-1950s, she took a job as the social events coordinator at the United States Naval Mission in Bogotá. She was basically the "party girl", coordinating big galas and social events for the small group of US Naval Officers and staff there to train the Colombian Navy. That's how she met Dad.

He was 34 years old and had no idea where Colombia was until he got his orders. He landed in Bogotá on June 21, 1958, where Mom met him on the tarmac, still a little groggy from a big event the previous night. Ironically, that would be the same day that Barb and I would marry 28 years later. Mom and Dad married just six months after they met. Dad was very practical and intentional, and Mom was a hard charger. Her way won out.

Mom stayed working at the mission for the remaining four years they were in Bogotá. When Dad got orders for Norfolk, VA in 1962, she said goodbye to family and friends and made the transition to becoming an American wife.

My birth in 1964 kept Mom focused on her role as a mother and out of the workforce. After our move to Oak Harbor, WA in 1969 and the start of my school years, she began to immerse herself in social events and volunteer projects.

Mom was ubiquitous around Oak Harbor. Dad used to joke that he was known not as Don Weedin, but as "Alicia's husband." My memory of those times is vivid. Mom was high-energy, incredibly smart, and easily bored if she wasn't doing something with a purpose or fun.

Those memories became even more prominent as I watched her slowly and steadily decline mentally. Over the last four years of her life, dementia robbed her of her personality and her most recent memories. She stopped speaking of Dad, because she literally forgot that he lived. Frontal lobe dementia attacks more recent memory, so after a while she was "living" in Bogotá in the 1940s and 50s—often confusing me for her brother Jaime.

One of my most emotional moments came the next-to-last-time I saw her awake before she passed. For years she had stopped referring to me as "Danny." She either didn't call me anything or called me Jimmy, thinking I was her brother. As I rolled her wheelchair into the dining hall for dinner before I left, she spoke to the woman sitting next to her at the table. Always the hostess, she pointed to me and exclaimed to the lady, "This is my son." And then repeated it for good measure.

I will never forget that moment—hopefully—as long as I live.

Family Matters
Family is something I took for granted for a long time. I mistakenly conjectured that everyone had a stress-free, middle-class upbringing where you were loved and encouraged by parents.

Make no mistake, I now understand that I was blessed and beyond lucky. The difficult stories related to my parents don't come until the end of their lives, due to illnesses outside of their control. Everything else before that was basically a Norman Rockwell painting.

That being said, family isn't without its own sand traps and water hazards.

On the Back Nine journey, we have a fascinating intersection of past and future. The story that begins this chapter signifies the past—where our parents are in their own final holes, often in a state of decline that is heartbreaking and emotional. After this chapter, I will share an *Out of the Bunker* narrative with commentary on how to navigate this often challenging time, based on my experiences.

The future for us is the next generation.

Not all of us will have grandchildren on the Back Nine walk, but for those of us that do, the experience is indescribable. That unique confluence is a dynamic that brings about a lot of emotions and perspective.

The Future

"Mommy, Pops is trying to say Halloween, but he's not getting it."

These words were said with pure exasperation by my 4-year-old granddaughter, Ellie. We were on a video call discussing that she and her sister Maddie would be staying with us over the Halloween weekend. I had long before cleverly renamed the day HalloWeedin. Ellie was having none of it.

After a brief back and forth where I tried in vain to induce her to embrace my "ingenious" term, she finally had enough and voiced her irritation to her mom. As a father of two daughters and a grandfather of two little girls, I've been on the other end of many an eye roll and aggravation.

The good news is that Ellie finally came over to my way of thinking and now proudly proclaims HalloWeedin as the official name of the day to go out dressed as a dinosaur and receive candy from strangers!

So, what about you?

While my interaction with Ellie is humorous, it does bring home the point that families are susceptible to exasperation, annoyance, and anger when the channels of communication fall apart.

Unlike friends and associates, you can't completely divorce yourself from family. Even at its worst, the memories linger, and at times this can be painful.

You don't need me to explain the dynamics involved. The factors in any family are an integration of love and hate (which I suggest might be the same thing at times), joys and sorrows shared, pain and guilt, and that singular familial balance of power among siblings.

The crux of complications comes from a breakdown in communications and clarity.

When it comes to non-family members, it's amazing how often we can find ways to be more patient, more empathetic, and less judgmental. We also are more able to filter our responses and walk away from a situation.

With families, not so much. The dynamics of our relationships sit atop a powder keg of emotions. When you throw in the "heat" of certain topics, the potential for a big bang is increased.

What are those powder kegs? You know them—religion, politics, outside relationships. Throw in a variety of personalities with that edge of history, and, well, you have a dynamite factory.

Dad and I certainly had our share of meltdowns when I was younger. He and I were wired differently. Dad was a processor—a deep thinker, analytic, and averse to change. I inherited Mom's Colombian zeal, along with a solid dose of impulsiveness, risk taking, energy, impatience, and boldness.

As I grew (and matured) into my mid-30s, those blowups dissipated to the point that they stopped occurring. I'd like to think that we both figured out how to better talk to each other. That being said, how we are wired never changes, and in the later years, I had to find a better way to influence.

Dad didn't do change well. As my role became more parental in the sense of managing their well-being as they got older, I ran into some roadblocks with him. There were decisions that needed to be made regarding what projects he should continue to do around the house, going to the doctor, and even driving.

It didn't take long for me to realize that it was not hard to dip back into the old way of presenting my arguments. Dad would literally get angry and shut down, and then I'd get angry and yell a lot.

Fortunately, I had matured and advanced in my communication skills.

I changed my approach with Dad. I knew he needed time to process and think. I started emailing him ideas for his consideration. I'd clearly lay out my idea with the reasons behind it. There was always an outcome that benefitted him and Mom— even if the change was uncomfortable on the surface. I'd email him on a Monday and tell him we could talk about it when we got together for our weekly lunch on Thursday. It never got that far.

Somewhere between that Monday and Thursday, he'd call me to say that he and Mom considered the idea and they concurred. There sometimes was a hint of understanding that things were changing—like when I told him I thought he should hire someone to take care of the yard. But this process of communication worked.

The Practice Range:

Family is incredibly important in our lives, and the Back Nine heightens that as we lose and add members along the way.

While I often hear and read where people agree with this principle, in practice the communications can get difficult.

Here are five ideas for you to process in your communication and clarity with family:

1. **If you don't agree on religion or politics, agree not to discuss these topics.** The truth is that you won't change any minds and it's not worth the fight. If you see social media posts that you don't like or with which you don't agree, let them go or just hide your feelings. You are all better served, mentally and emotionally.

2. **Same book, different chapter.** Find the common goal. I've witnessed situations where there appears to be disengagement on an issue. The knee-jerk reaction is that people are on the metaphorical "different page".

My wife Barb has an excellent observation on this. She opines that it's more about being in the same book—just a different chapter. The common goal—that shared desired outcome—is "the book". Based on experiences and preferences, others might be on a different chapter.

For example: Siblings desire the very best for their parents as they age. That's the book. Points of view on housing, medical care, driving, and activities all may be different and emotional. Those are the chapters. When there can be accord on the book and respect and flexibility within the chapters, the chance that we all eventually land on the same page is improved.

3. **Understand how people are wired.** After a while, I came to understand how Dad was "wired". Same goes for my wife of over 35 years, my children, and most of my close, extended family. It's taken me a long time—I can be a slow learner! Now I try to do my best to prepare for important conversations. This is not intended to be deceptive or manipulative: it's meant to improve the

understanding for everyone and to find common ground and solutions.

My approach is that it's incumbent on me—not on anyone else—to change communication styles. It goes back to, "My ball, my destiny". It's what I can control to better all experiences.

4. **Be prepared to end a conversation without a conclusion.** Yes, we all want closure. But sometimes it's better to simply leave when no clear path is evident. Depending on the family member, that might mean sleeping on it or taking an extended hiatus.

5. **Protect your mental health.** Situations can be fraught with high emotion. Outside of your spouse, significant other, and children, the stress is often not worth the fight. There's that old axiom about knowing what hill to die on. I contend there is no hill worth *dying on for you.*

Captain Jack on the Green

I don't think any sentient being (I'm a Jack Russel—I'm smart, okay) does family better than dogs.

We don't judge. We don't care about what you said in anger before. We don't manipulate (other than when it's time to eat, but who doesn't!). We don't have hidden agendas. We only use one word.

All we want is someone to love us and be loved by us.

When Dan coached basketball, he said he only had one rule. That rule was: "Don't let your teammates down". That's pithy, yet powerful. We dogs won't ever let you down—at least not on purpose. And, if we do (like that time when I accidentally got into the garbage), we are genuinely sorry.

Maybe that's what humans should make as a rule for families.

Don't let your teammates down in what you do or say.

There. That was easy.

Captain Jack out...

It's been seven years since Mom passed away at the age of 90. I still remember the phone call at 11:30 pm that starts with the lady on the other end saying, *"I'm very sorry to inform you …"*

That moment was bittersweet. It was difficult losing Mom just days after I turned half a century old. Yet it also marked the end of a tumultuous four years where dementia robbed her and us of who she really was. And, during the first two years of that journey, Barb and I were her caregivers while she lived at our home.

I made tons of mistakes. I could be bitter, angry, frustrated, and loud in my expression of those emotions. Hell, I could be really mean to her. I still deal with guilt. Time has helped, but I wish I knew then what I now better understand today.

I know many people reading this book are somewhere on this journey with their parents. For those of you in the midst of this— or who one day will be—allow me to share a few confessions:

1. **I wish I'd left my pride at the door.** Way too often, I argued with Mom over "facts". I was right, but she had dementia! In twenty minutes, she would forget the argument; for me it lasted hours, if not days. But for that time, I made her unhappy and made me miserable. It was later when she

was in the memory care facility, that I finally figured out that I didn't need to be right; I needed to be better.

2. **I wish I had sought professional help.** I could have used counseling or therapy. That would have helped me be more perceptive. After Mom went into memory care, Barb and I joined a support group at the facility. It was easily one of the best decisions we made. It wasn't as if I shunned getting help. I literally just didn't think about it.

3. **I wish I had more fun.** The two years Mom lived with us were not all hard. Barb worked outside the home at the time, so I was home a lot with Mom—even when we had help coming in to be with her. I remember playing games, taking walks, and watching television together. In hindsight, investing more in that fun time would have been nice.

4. **I wish we'd made the decision to move her to memory care earlier.** At the beginning, it was best to have her in our home and bring in help. However, the last six months she spent with us were more than challenging. To put it simply, Barb and I were above our paygrade. We had to sleep with our bedroom door open to make sure that when Mom got up at night to use the bathroom, she would safely traverse the path to and from with her walker. It was harder than having a baby or toddler. The

move was a difficult decision, but after the initial, hard transition, it was one of the most freeing experiences I had. I was "fired" as her caregiver and able to go back to simply being her son.

While there are more, that's it for now. Maybe I will write a full book on this topic. For now, just know that at some point in all of our Back Nine walks, this is a likely hazard waiting for us to play through.

The 13th Hole: Friends

Jumanji

It was the 18th hole at Homestead Golf Course in Lynden, WA—a nice resort-style golf venue near the Canadian border. This was the finishing hole of the final round of our annual tournament called Jumanji.

In 1996, a bunch of us from high school started this annual tradition. We were all golfers—although many came to the game after high school. We were all about 31 years old at that time and eager to find a reason to get together to play a whole bunch of golf.

The title came from the movie of the same name[3], starring the late, great Robin Williams. We figured that five rounds of golf (ninety holes) over two-and-a-half days was the equivalent of walking through the jungle!

This started as a small group of eight people. Over the past twenty-six events, we've had about fifteen guys who've participated. In a normal year, between eight to twelve people will play. There's a core group of us that have played most years. I've personally played in twenty-two of the twenty-six.

---

[3] "Jumanji," IMDb.com, https://www.imdb.com/title/tt0113497/

Regardless of how many times you show up, once you're in Jumanji, you're one of the boys forever.

That first year, I remember walking all ninety holes. My feet were obliterated at the end. Soon it morphed into walking the first eighteen and then carting the second. Not long after, we carted every round. And after about year fifteen (when I was 46 years old), we dropped a round and limited the event to seventy-two holes.

Standing on the 18th hole with about 125 yards to a green guarded by water, I appropriately chose my 9-iron. This was the exact right club for the distance on a balmy summer day.

I stood over the ball and then confidently swung. I made excellent contact. As soon as the ball was in flight, my cart buddy Rick exclaimed, *"Wow, nice shot!"*

The ball was heading straight at the pin, but something was off. Instead of hitting an arc where it should have started its descent, the ball kept rising. And rising. And rising.

The ball cleared the green and caromed off the roof of the tall clubhouse. It bounded back down the roof, making the loud, clanging sound that every golfer dreads because it means their golf ball was bounding on someone's roof.

"What the f***?!" was all I could blurt out. Rick was already laughing in the cart.

I looked down at the club wondering what had just happened. Then I saw it ...

A 6-iron.

You see a 6-iron has the same markings on the clubhead as a 9-iron—only upside down. The clubmakers properly show a line underneath the "6" to make sure stupid golfers wouldn't mistake it for a 9-iron. It's a longer club, which somehow also evaded me. And it's a club that when well-struck will carry thirty yards further than the 9-iron.

I repeated the expletive and included a few extra for good measure. By this time, Rick was laughing uncontrollably.

The incident has become one of many stories that have become part of the lore of Jumanji. Rick reminded me of it again just last summer and this happened at least a decade ago.

Golf is a game that will humble you. The more memorable stories are the ones that come at the expense of our lack of skill or judgment in a particular moment.

To this day, I always look twice when I want to hit either a 6- or 9-iron.

What Club Are You Playing?

Picking the right club is necessary for good shots and scores. Sometimes we choose wrong by a lot (as in my example). Sometimes we miss by only a little. The more times we pick the right club and execute the proper swing, the better our score will be.

And as we get older, our club selection will also change. Even the best golfers in the world will eventually lose some yardage due to age, injury, and loss of flexibility or strength. Adjustments need to be made to play successfully.

It's no different than picking friends.

It's rare to keep the same level of friendships over the span of years. Distance can be the biggest factor, although technology has eased that a bit to at least allow for improved ability to stay in touch.

However, just as in golf, we need to be vigilant of the "club selection" as we grow into different parts of life. The same people we hung out with in our youth may not be the same we should be hanging out with now. And that's not a judgment on character; it's more about commonality and energy.

Rotary

I joined Rotary in November 1993 at 28 years old. At that time—and it's still true today—that was a really young age. The average age of Rotarians in any given club is in the high 50s or early 60s. Heck, I've been a Rotarian for damn near 30 years and I'm still in the "young" group!

Rotary has been an integral part of my life. Outside of the rewards of giving back to the community—both local and international—many of my best friendships have come from fellow members. The people I most regularly hang out with at the golf course, the bar, and at each other's homes are Rotarians. I'd wager that about 90% of the business that I acquired over those nearly three decades originated in some way through my association with Rotary.

The beauty of this association is that friends have continually been added over the years as new members have joined. Friends, like family, also have transitions. Some friends have left the club and, while we are still friends, we don't see each other as often. In a similar vein, some have left Rotary, but we forged such a strong friendship through commonalities and energy that we've made the friendship a priority.

Commonality and energy

We humans need friends. If you're like me, your closest friends may be more "family" than members of your family.

The reasons are commonality and energy.

We pick our friends at the start because we have something in common. In grade school, junior high, and high school, for me it was sports that bonded us. It then became common experiences. If you've ever played a team sport, you understand the bond that comes from sharing the best and most painful experiences together.

That commonality remains through life—church community, young adult groups, Lamaze class, puppy training classes, co-workers, service groups, military, etc.

Sometimes that commonality wanes, and sometimes it just gets lost for a variety of reasons. It can't be forced. When commonality is still strong, then the foundation of a friendship will remain.

As we mature, I believe *energy* is more important than ever.

Who in your circle of friends gives you energy? Or maybe the better question is—who doesn't?

We can't pick our family, but we can certainly choose the friends with whom we invest our time. While commonality is the foundation, energy is the lifeline. We are all wired differently, and that's a good thing. But because of that, the power of energy is different. Some people connect, and others just don't.

And because of individual experiences, sometimes that energy level is diminished.

Here's the deal. I've made a conscious decision at this stage of my life to, as much as I can control, be friends with people that provide energy—not indifference or aggravation. That includes my friends and the people who I want to be clients. The metaphorical course is too short.

You should, too.

Jumanji – Next Gen
In the beginning, Jumanji was about the golf.

It was about playing as many holes in as many different venues for as long as we could go. Or at least that's what I thought.

Now golf is simply the vehicle. It's the common activity that continues to bring us together. What keeps us together is the energy that we bring each other that's manifested in smiles, laughter (especially at each other), sharing meals with a few adult beverages, and the memories that span, in some cases, over fifty years.

We may have all grown up in the same city, but over time our life experiences and world views are different. But at least for this group, it doesn't matter. While we may be varied in perspectives and opinions, it's not a part of our shared friendship. There's mutual respect and trust that permeates the group (except on the golf course!).

It doesn't matter where we travel to play; it doesn't matter even how we play. It now only matters that we show up. I've been fortunate to have had this group of friends nearly my whole life. Golf is the conduit.

A special, personal note of thanks to my Jumanji brothers: Lee, Rick, Richard, Kevin B., Ron, Doug, Scott, Ray, Jay, Jim G., Corey, Eric, Paul, Marc, Kevin C., and Jim M. (RIP).

The Practice Range:

Who's your Jumanji?

I know there are extroverts and introverts. However, humans need other humans. I suggest that extroverts may likely have a higher capacity for greater numbers of friends, but introverts still need a few.

I acknowledge that family members are friends. Yet wouldn't you agree that there is a deep-seated need for people outside your inner familial circle?

I can golf with just about anyone. It's only eighteen holes, right? But for me to call someone "friend" and to invest time and energy into that friendship for the Back Nine, well, that requires a fair share of commonality and energy. And as a serial extrovert, I've got capacity!

I challenge you to take a close look at your best friends.

Have you become so mired in your business or career that you don't have many friends?

Have you hung on too long to some friends who no longer give you energy (and likewise you may not give to them) from sheer sameness? Has boredom set in?

Do you seek out new friends that share something in common?

Do you have "old" friends with whom you'd like to get re-acquainted?

Facebook has its issues, make no mistake. However, it's been a wonderful place for me to renew friendships, both virtually and in person. Technology can be a great tool to help advance friendships when utilized well.

We all need friends to walk the course with us. You can choose how many you have. Just make sure they are the kind that will laugh with you when you hit your golf ball on the roof!

Captain Jack on the Green

Bella and I have glommed on to a bunch of Dan and Barb's friends. They call them neighbors.

Dan said that back when he was a kid, the neighbors all knew each other and were friends. They talked a lot, shared food, had barbecues, and a whole bunch of other stuff. He says not everyone has that. He said it was special.

He says our neighbors are special, too. We always see them when we are out for walks. They say hello and always smile at us. Some of them even have other dogs. Bella isn't very friendly to the other dogs. She barks at them. Dan has to always apologize and explain that she's a "diva". I don't know what that means but I think its code for "loud".

The neighbors get together a lot out on Scott's grassy area. It's the big corner lawn that is an easy spot for everyone to gather. Personally, I like to pee on his bushes that guard the grass, but don't tell anyone.

Dan says all the neighbors are friends because we like to do things with them and always are there to lend a hand.

The neighbors are my friends, too. Even the other dogs.

Captain Jack out ...

The 14th Hole: Travel

Where are you from?

> ❝ *Travel is fatal to prejudice, bigotry, and narrow-mindedness, and many of our people need it sorely on these accounts. Broad, wholesome, charitable views of men and things cannot be acquired by vegetating in one little corner of the earth all one's lifetime.* [4]
>
> ~ Mark Twain

I admit that travel is a huge priority for Barb and me in our Back Nine Walk. I've travelled quite a bit within the United States and Canada, but outside of that, I've only been to Colombia on five different occasions.

We're eager to visit Europe, Asia, Australia, and other places around the globe. While the pandemic is making that trickier than before, it's still a priority.

Our family has been deeply impacted by travel. While we may not have the scope of travel that we wish, my association with Rotary International has significantly affected our worldview for the

---

[4] Mark Twain Quotes, Brainyquote.com,
https://www.brainyquote.com/quotes/mark_twain_1063866

better. Because of the Rotary Youth Exchange program, we feel like we've been all around the globe.

Since 1994, Barb and I have hosted nine exchange students in our home. I've been a Youth Exchange Counselor and Officer for our club, and I now sit on the District Youth Exchange committee.

We've learned the cultures of so many countries from those who have lived with us and whom we have had as part of our lives. Most specifically, we are grateful to the following people for sharing their cultures and worldviews with us:

- Alfredo from Argentina in 1994-95
- Brice from France in 2000-01
- Oscar from Denmark from 2001-02
- Maru from Venezuela from 2003-04
- Michael from Switzerland in 2008-09
- Juhi from India in 2009-10
- Tati from Colombia in 2011-12
- Cristy from Ecuador in 2012-23
- Leo from Germany in 2019-20

There were so many others that impacted our lives during my time as a counselor and exchange officer: Nike from Hungary; Sidney from The Netherlands, Archie from Nigeria, Katri from Finland, Giacomo (Jack) from Italy, and Duda from Brazil.

These people became like sons and daughters to Barb and me. For my daughters, they were big (and then little) brothers and sisters.

Through each of them, we experienced their cultures while sharing ours. We enjoyed a variety of new foods (Indian food is hot—very hot), shared in their own country's holiday traditions (in Brazil, you wear white on New Year's), spent time conversing with their parents and siblings, and even were gifted clothes from their society (I now fit much better into my Nigerian shirt).

When our daughter Mindy was in Europe for a college semester, she traveled by plane, train, and automobile to Denmark to visit Oscar and his wife. He had been a big brother to her. And when Barb and I were visiting my family in Colombia, we journeyed to visit Tati in her hometown of Paipa to spend a few days with her family.

My family in Colombia has also been instrumental in my growth and understanding of cultures and communities outside of my own. To all of them, I'm beyond grateful.

So, what does this all mean for you?

We can't go through our lives trapped in our own little bubble. While there may be impediments to allowing us to physically travel around the world, there are other ways to still "travel".

The ability to meet people virtually, to exchange ideas, and to gain understanding is an important component of humanity.

The Beaten Path

I recently met a gentleman who holds the distinction of visiting all 3,068 counties, parishes, and boroughs in the United States. He accomplished this over a nine-and-a-half-year period between 1986 and 1995.

My goal is to get to all fifty states, the District of Columbia, and Puerto Rico. I've got twenty-nine states and D.C. in the bank. I've been fortunate to have the opportunity to speak and have clients in many of these states.

Travel doesn't have to be international to have a cultural impact. The United States is certainly a diverse country. Visiting many of its different parts can be comparable to visiting a foreign country.

I've had the privilege of driving through New York City and Beaver Falls, PA. I've eaten in a historical restaurant in Newport, RI and a sports bar in Fargo, ND. I'm sure you all have your own travel experiences as well.

My point is that travel is necessary for perspective, empathy, and understanding. Ultimately, if world peace is what we all want— and at least that's what we *seem* to say we want—then travel outside of the "little corner of the Earth" should be a priority.

The Practice Range:

Travel is a pastime to which Barb and I are committed—perhaps as much selfishly as for any other reason. We want to see places and meet people and enjoy that time of travel together. For us, the shared experience is most meaningful.

Notably, one of my promises to Barb is to go to the place of her birth, Argentia, Newfoundland. Barb was born on the US Naval Base in Argentia, and has almost no recollection of her short time there before her dad was transferred to Jacksonville, FL.

She held a dual citizenship with Canada until she was 18 years old, when she had to make a decision. At that time, she had to declare her allegiance to one country, and she chose the United States.

One of her Back Nine dreams is to visit the place of her birth, and I'm excited to join her. Maybe we can swing by Norfolk, VA as we make the turn back for home to see where I was born!

What about you?

I know travel isn't for everyone for a variety of reasons. However, I firmly believe we miss out on a lot in building our own perspectives if we forego the opportunity to advance our awareness of other humans and their lives.

Captain Jack on the Green

I don't get to go anywhere outside of the neighborhood. That's my travel.

However, I've had many friends stay at my house while I've lived there. Let me see.

There was Mike from Switzerland. He accidentally left the screen door open as he was leaving for the movies with a friend. I dashed out the front door and into the beautiful, chilled night. It was awesome. I let Dan catch me after I had some fun.

There was Juhi from India. I got away from her, too ,when some kid came selling something at the front door and she was home from school. She was smart. She went and got a cookie and lured me back with it. She is way smarter than Dan. Maybe that's why she's a doctor today.

There was Tati from Colombia. She used to be very nice to me by letting me sit with her while she rubbed the back of my ears and said things like, "Ohhhh, Captain Jaack." She's a doctor now, too.

Then there was Cristy from Ecuador. Cristy liked to make art and I liked to watch her do it. I was jealous because I have no fingers and couldn't help.

There was Leo from Germany. He played the piano. He was amazing. Bella and I loved to listen to him practice. We have a piano in the house, but Dan doesn't know how to use it. Luckily, Leo did and played for us!

But wait ... there were more ...

I met Nike from Hungary. She went to see the Wizard of Oz at the Seattle Symphony in Seattle with Grandma Alicia.

I met Archie from Nigeria. He brought Dan and Barb cool African shirts from his home.

I met Katri from Finland. She told me about how all dogs in Finland have their own sauna. I want one.

I met Sidney from The Netherlands. She liked to come over and rub behind my ears. She was always smiling.

I met Jack from Italy. I love his name. He was very funny. Just like me. He even gave Dan a Lego Captain Jack!

I met Duda from Brazil. She came over to the house before Homecoming to take pictures. She was going to teach me to swim but we never got around to it. She bought a dog in Brazil to make up for it.

So, I guess I have travelled quite a bit. I've been to Switzerland, India, Colombia, Ecuador, and Germany, plus some side trips to Hungary, Nigeria, Finland, The Netherlands, Italy, and Brazil.

Pretty good for a dog, don't you think?

Captain Jack out ...

It was Jumanji 1998. I was on the 9th hole at Desert Canyon, near Wenatchee.

The 9th hole looks out over a canyon. I will always remember standing on the tee and peering out at one of the meanest and most spine-chilling looking clouds I'd ever seen.

As my cart buddy Eric and I were rolling down the 9th fairway, it became clear that the cloud was moving faster than we were. We made the turn and made it as far as the 11th tee. And then it hit... hard.

One of the craziest and scariest drives I've ever experienced was in the golf cart heading back up the 10th fairway as water was rushing against us. Eric was driving the cart and we were skidding and hydroplaning all the way back to the clubhouse.

By the time we got indoors, everyone was soaked. I'm not sure I've ever been wetter in my life. We were literally dripping puddles of water at our feet.

As is the case in deserts, the storm was brief. After about thirty minutes, the sun came out and the course was dry enough to let people back out. Almost all the other golfers that day had already left. Of the twelve of us playing, only one group—the four guys who were in the running for the coveted trophy—went back out.

The rest of our group left, except for two people—Ron and me. We had no interest in playing any more (we were THAT wet still), but we had to stay because we were riding with one of the guys who was back out on the course!

After eating lunch, we figured it was pointless to sit in soggy clothes. Ron went out to his car to get a change of clothes, and I walked out to the car that had my stuff. And then it hit me like the earlier rain ...

My brother-in-law Kevin—who was out playing and eventually won the event—had the keys to the car. While Ron was waiting for his passenger to return, I WAS the passenger. That ensuing two hours were miserable.

The moral of the story: When and wherever you travel in life, be ready for the rain, both before and after.

The 15ᵗʰ Hole: Wealth

Dan's Nine Rules of Wealth

(Because sometimes you only have time for nine holes)

Golf is full of rules.

If you are even just an occasional player, you must be aware of both the written and unwritten rules of any game you play. And, unlike any other sport, you must be prepared to call an infraction on yourself and suffer the consequences of penalty strokes or laughter at your expense.

I will preface by saying I'm not a financial planner or wealth manager. If you think I will be advising on your stock portfolio, you will be disappointed!

I've created my own personal rules of wealth. They are broken up into three categories of three rules each, based on how I define wealth:

- Spiritual
- Financial
- Health & Wellness

Spiritual

Rule 1: You've Got Spirit—Yes You Do

We all have a spirit within us, so use it. While I've been a practicing Catholic from the cradle, I certainly acknowledge and respect everyone's right to a faith and religion. This faith includes being agnostic or atheist.

But everyone also contains a spirit of life. As we walk the Back Nine of life, that spirit is needed more than ever to produce joy, wonder, curiosity, perspective, and ultimately self-awareness.

Rule 2: Seek to Find

I find my spirituality within my faith, whether that be at Mass, or by study through reading, listening, or watching.

To maximize your spiritual life—however that might look—you must seek it out. That might be through quiet meditation, in nature, or with your most cherished relationships. For all I know, you might find it walking down the fairways.

Be intentional on this—even if it is only in small doses. A small dose goes a long way to serenity within your spirit.

Rule 3: Be Not Afraid

My observation is that many people are fearful of expressing their spirit. That fear takes many forms, both internally and externally. The most common is avoidance. This is an intentional act to dodge judgment from both others and one's self.

I surmise that many folks are reticent to appear enthusiastic about their own personal spirituality, as they may have witnessed others being overly zealous.

My rule here is that it's okay to give yourself permission to be who you are. The caveat is that at the same time, you need to give that same respect to those who choose a different path. The Back Nine is often a journey of faith and spirit: Let's allow everyone to walk at their own pace and path.

Financial

Rule 4: Get a Caddy

Unless you're a professional financial or wealth adviser, go find someone to help you with your money. Period.

You have more important things to do—like make the money to invest. Allow that trusted advisor to help you manage it.

Rule 5: If You're In the Rough, Get Back Into Play

There's an unwritten course management rule I now try to use. I wish I had done it earlier in life!

If I'm hitting out of the deep rough or in the woods, my mantra is don't be stupid. Get back into play in one shot. That takes double bogey out of the equation.

We all get into deep rough financially at some point for a variety of reasons. Life is that way. My non-professional advice is the same as the golf course: Get back into play as quickly as you can.

And this advice corresponds with Rule #4. Find someone to hand you the right club (code for tools, resources, and guidance) to wedge your way out of trouble and back on the fairway.

Rule 6: Fuel Your Life

My colleague and good friend Phil Symchych often writes and advises that money is the fuel for life.[5] I've made this a rule to remember.

While acknowledging that proper financial planning includes budgeting, saving, and investing, there is more to life than being scared to use your money to enjoy it.

Unlike on an actual golf course, we never know when the Back Nine will suddenly end. That's why we should thoughtfully invest time in creating a lifestyle plan that includes spouse, significant

---

[5] Phil Symchych and Alan Weiss, *The Business Wealth Builders*, (Business Expert Press, 2015).

other, and loved ones. Make sure you budget some of that hard earned income to enjoy the lifestyle that you want.

Oscar Wilde, one of my favorite humorists, is quoted as saying, *"Anyone who lives within their means suffers from a lack of imagination."*[6] While my financial advisor friends might not agree with the "within their means" part, I think we all get where Mr. Wilde is going with this.

Health & Wellness

Rule 7: Be Strong

My personal fitness coach Brett Clark has an interesting viewpoint when it comes to health in the United States. He says, "We don't have an obesity problem: we have a strength problem."[7]

In other words, while not minimizing the choices we make as far as eating, Brett feels like we are losing muscle and strength as we age—to the detriment of everything else related to our physical health.

When it comes to "health wealth", we control almost all of the factors leading to how wealthy we are. Just like golf, it's our ball

---

[6] Oscar Wilde quotes, Goodreads.com,
https://www.goodreads.com/author/quotes/3565.Oscar_Wilde
[7] Brett Clark, BC Fitness Studio, https://bcfitstudio.com/

and our destiny. Unfortunately, as a society we've gotten weak. But as an individual, you can change it.

Similar to my rule on financial wealth, I implore you to do what my family has done and get an expert to guide you. On the Back Nine, our bodies change—sometimes dramatically —regardless of how fit we are. I injured my shoulder boxing on a heavy bag because I was improperly punching.

I knew how to train and exercise on the Front Nine of my game (or more likely, I thought I did). On the Back Nine, it was clear that I was hurting myself, as I was less physically strong than before. What was most important was to get to a position with my strength and fitness where I could avoid getting hurt playing golf, continue playing with my granddaughters, and age gracefully. And I know I couldn't do it alone.

Bottom line: Find an expert that will tailor a plan for you to get stronger and fitter. Health is a wealth that you don't want to find in a state of bankruptcy in your final holes. Your investment now will keep you on par for the duration.

P.S. Studies show that regular exercise in mid-life can significantly reduce the risk of developing dementia by 30% and

Alzheimer's Disease by 45%.[8] Now there's some great investment advice!

Rule 8: Eat Better, Damnit!

You all know this. It's one of those oddities where we all KNOW the answer to better health, but are often willing to eschew that knowledge and chew on a candy bar while swigging a soda pop for a midday snack (and a diet soda is just as bad).

Food is the fuel for our bodies to function. Period.

While we also enjoy the flavor and fun that comes with food, the primary part of our health wealth rests with what we opt to consume. The adage *you are what you eat* is absolute truth.

This is another investment in our long-term health wealth. We know that poor eating habits lead to maladies as we age, like hypertension, cardiovascular disease, cancer, gout, and dementia, to name a few.

I'm not talking about dieting. What I've developed is an intentional eating plan. It's not a fad; it's not for a short time. It's an actual game plan that is meant to allow me to have flexibility

---

[8] Reference: https://www.alzheimers.org.uk/about-dementia/risk-factors-and-prevention/physical-exercise

78

and balance to allow me to walk the Back Nine instead of having to ride in a cart.

Here is my simple plan:

- **Control portions**. This one was tough. Now, I rarely take seconds. I get what I want the first time around. I've got some flexibility for special occasions, but 90% is one-and-done.

- **Eat more veggies**. This is a new priority for me. I don't love vegetables, but I've made consuming them—even if I must hide them in a smoothie—a part of my overall plan.

- **Organic**. Yeah, organic costs more, and I know there are naysayers out there. Naysay away. For me, I'm going to avoid the chance of whatever chemicals are being used to artificially lengthen the shelf life of food, so it doesn't shorten my own life.

- **Minimize processed foods**. It's almost impossible to completely avoid processed foods. That being said, we absolutely can control how much—or how little—we eat them. When I must use processed foods, they are organic and low in salt, sugar, and chemicals.

- **Hydrate.** I quantify this one—90 ounces of water a day. That doesn't include my 20 ounces of coffee in the morning, or my libation or glass of wine at night. Hydration becomes more important as we age, and we actually get worse at it! My mother hated drinking water when she was older because she didn't want to go to the bathroom as much! Drink water. Go to the bathroom more. It will be good for you!

- **Wine and Whiskey.** You don't have to include this, but I do. I enjoy a libation at the end of the day or a glass of beautiful red wine with my dinner. Notice I used the singular for both. One libation or one glass of wine. Certainly, there are occasions when an extra is warranted, but the rule is one.

- **Have fun.** I love good food. I love wine and spirits. I love to cook. I love sharing the food experience with family and friends. My plan is flexible enough to indulge on occasion, but then it's back to being on track. Food is a part of life and is meant to be enjoyed. Like everything else, moderation is the key. As we traverse the Back Nine, it's of even greater importance.

Rule 9: Take Care of Your Mentals

This is wisdom from that great American philosopher and former Seattle Seahawks star running back, Marshawn Lynch. Shortly after he retired, he counseled players to *"Take care of your chicken (code for money) and your mentals."*[9] We talked chicken earlier in this chapter, now let's dig into the mentals!

We've witnessed and heard brave people reveal how they had to confront their own mental health issues. While the most prominent have come from recognizable names from the celebrity world—like athletes, artists, and entertainers—make no mistake that we non-celebrities are at as much risk of needing to be aware of our own mentals.

In my lifetime, this concern over mental health has never had this attention. In fact, I contend there was a time in the not-too-distant past when it was considered a weakness to need mental health counseling or therapy. People feared being judged by others and even of judging themselves.

In business, employers must be attuned and empathetic to the challenges employees may be facing. Employees must do the same for their bosses. Let's face it. We have faced, and will always continue to face, challenging times for businesses due to a variety of reasons.

---

[9] Marshawn Lynch: https://www.nbcsports.com/northwest/seattle-seahawks/marshawn-lynch-his-younger-seahawks-teammates-take-care-yall-chicken

On the personal front, we have family, friends, and community members that are all likely dealing with something. We just don't know it. Kindness and understanding go a long way towards being supportive. Of important note, that includes kindness and support to ourselves by taking care of our own mentals first.

The Practice Range:

My colleague and good friend Brad Berger is both a financial advisor and life coach. He firmly believes (and I agree) that we all have the capability to live to a hundred years old and beyond. The data bears this out.

In a country that has an educated population, medical and technology advancements, access to care and insurance, and access to clean water and good food, a person who reaches the age of 65 years has a life expectancy of 93 years old.

That means we need to make sure we have addressed all three levels of wealth that I have outlined—spiritual, financial, and health and wellness.

Now is the time to invest in all three. What can you start today—right now—that you aren't doing already? Don't make it difficult. Pick at least one item from each category and improve it. Then rinse and repeat.

Captain Jack on the Green

I'm rich.

That's right, I'm upper class, baby. I've got free food, free rent, and free health care for life.

That may sound good—and it is—but I am rich in other ways. I get up every morning and seek out new adventures. The lawn may look the same, but there's something new out there and I'm going to find it—especially if it's a snake. I'm not worried about yesterday or tomorrow. I go as the spirit moves me.

I walk just about every day—even in the rain. I don't always love it, but I know that it's good for me. I also get to strut my stuff for the lady dogs! And the other guy dogs—they look at me and say, "Now that's a cool dog!"

Yeah, I'm lucky not to have to worry about money, but there is way more to wealth than that. Being truly rich like me starts in your head. Or, perhaps in your tail.

Captain Jack out ...

Making money is sexy. Insurance—not so much. Until you need it to protect your hard-earned wealth and lifestyle, and then it becomes essential.

As a follow-through on the financial segment of the previous chapter, allow me to wax poetic on the forms of insurances you need to assure the lifestyle of you and the ones you love.

Life Insurance:

I can't imagine in the history of the world that any beneficiary of life insurance proceeds declined the money by telling the insurance company, *"Nah, I don't need this much money."*

Any death at any time will cause some level of financial consequence to those left behind. There can be fear of not being able to maintain a lifestyle, or even keep up a property. There will be stress in paying for final expenses. There might be fear of future college plans for children.

Unfortunately, life insurance is commonly viewed as an expense rather than an investment in someone else's future. Most people are underinsured for life insurance. You will never be younger or healthier than you are today. Make sure your loved ones will be free of fear and anxiety from your untimely passing.

Disability Insurance:

Disability Insurance is the one insurance product that protects an asset you don't already own – your future income.

You're more likely to become disabled before age 65 than to die. For most of us, that means the money machine stops operating. The same fear and stresses arise and may even be exacerbated, due to medical costs for care.

Invest in protecting your future income. The money you save might be your own.

Long-Term Care Insurance:

You've read the story of my parents. They didn't have Long-Term Care (LTC) Insurance (it really wasn't even available to them). Over the course of four years, we estimate the cost of their care combined was in excess of $500,000. It took their house and all their assets—to a point that Barb and I were covering most of Mom's monthly costs for the last years of her life.

I purchased my first LTC policy at 41 years old. After writing the first of several $10,000 monthly checks for the assisted living facility for my parents, I bought a second policy.

The costs for care are increasing exponentially. The likelihood of needing care is also rising as we are living longer. Even if you could self-fund the costs, why would you? The money you would lose from not being able to pursue more aggressive investments is worth the price of the premium. If you don't think you can afford the premium, then you can't afford the event.

That's why Barb and I have policies: to protect each other and to assure that our children won't be handed the financial consequences of not having adequate resources available.

I encourage any of you who don't currently have a plan to find a trusted advisor to have this discussion. It will be time and money well spent.

The 16th Hole: Mentoring

The Pep Girls

"Uno. Dos. Tres!"

This important countdown is proclaimed with gusto in unison among the two Pep Girls and me.

The Pep Girls are my granddaughters, Ellie and Maddie. Since Ellie was born, I've been hanging out every Thursday with them. We call it, "Thursdays with Pops."

In that timespan, which is now over four years, I've had to re-acquaint myself with the skills of diaper changing and lunch-making for toddlers. I've had to sharpen my debate and negotiation abilities, though I tend to be more Hamilton Burger than Perry Mason. (If you're still playing the Front Nine, you may have to Google the 1960s show, *Perry Mason*[10].)

Uno, Dos, Tres is a game we invented together when they were toddlers. Here's how it works.

Both girls get into Maddie's crib and throw all the stuffed animals out on to the floor in a big pile. I then grab a stuffie—and Ellie

---

[10] Perry Mason, IMDb: https://www.imdb.com/title/tt0050051/

tells me to whom it belongs—and then we count, "Uno, dos, tres." Then I toss the stuffie to the correct child for them to gleefully catch. Any deviation from this is *not* allowed. When all the stuffies are back in their corners, we repeat the process of "abandon crib" and do it all over again.

And so their Spanish lessons begin!

Mentoring

As we hit full stride in the Back Nine journey, we are put into positions to add value to the lives of others. By this point, our children are usually in at least the teen years, and often graduating high school and college, joining the military, or starting careers. Whether we like it or not, we've taken on a mentoring role.

Mentoring is defined in the dictionary as: "(in business) the practice of assigning a junior member of staff to the care of a more experienced person who assists him/her in their career."[11]

Mentoring is essential in any business. If you're the CEO or business owner, it's incumbent for your organization to set up mentoring opportunities for new people. Gone are the days of simply throwing people into the fray.

---

[11] Dictionary.com - https://www.dictionary.com/browse/mentoring

I still remember my first days as an insurance agent. I was given some writing implements, a desk, a bunch of rating manuals, and a hearty, *"Go get 'em and good luck!"* It was 1989, so no computer, no mobile phones, and I had to use an actual printed map to find places (some of you may have to Google that one, too!).

Staffing has been harder than ever in the aftermath of COVID-19. Potential employees expect more out of employers when it comes to skill acquisition and support, and they deserve as much.

I believe there's a clear delineation between mentoring and coaching.

Coaching is the acquisition of skills. You see it in athletics where a coach is hired to help forge a better golf swing, throw a baseball faster, tackle better in football, or become a better ball handler in basketball or soccer.

In business, we need coaches to help with both hard and soft skills. Coaches can help develop and improve the **hard skills**, like the better use of tools in machining or construction, how to drive a commercial vehicle, how to advance technology, and better sales development—to name a few.

Soft skills is an awful name. Soft seems to connote weak or unimportant. That's far from accurate. Savvy entrepreneurs, professionals, and executives hire coaches as advisors to improve their competence in areas such as communications, influence, and time management. Many times, changing behaviors is also part of the coaching process.

Mentoring is more reactive. A mentor is a guide and a place to find support and answers to questions as they arise. They might be better considered a confidante or trusted advisor.

Coaching should have a clear end period, because a skill or behavior should have changed. If not, the coaching didn't work. Mentoring can last much longer—even forever.

Businesses aren't the only organizations that can benefit from mentoring. My Rotary Club is probably not unique when it comes to assigning a mentor to new members. We found that to keep members more than a year, it's crucial to get them comfortable and engaged. The mentor program allows them to meet someone new (it's never the person that sponsored them), and to have an advocate to help them with questions about the club.

Your business experience is valuable to someone. Whether it's an employee, a co-worker, or a business associate, the activity of mentoring creates a positive experience for them and for you. I've mentored both as a volunteer and as a business advisor, and I am certain I've benefited just as much as the person I mentored—if not more.

You will, too.

Partners in Crime

It's not hard for me to get into trouble.

One Thursday evening, Mindy called me after having been with the Pep Girls. Her tone was a bit accusatory.

Mindy: "Were you and the girls sitting on the armrest of the sofa?'
Me: "Yes."
Mindy: "Why would you do that?"
Me: "I don't know." (You should be getting a sense of many of the conversations I've had with Barb, Mindy, and Kelli in my life.)
Mindy: "That's not allowed and now I heard that you've been teaching them to sit on the arm and then fall back onto the sofa."
Me: How did you find out? (Like I didn't already know!)
Mindy: "Ellie told me."
Me: "I was there to catch them. We were being safe."
Mindy: "Doesn't matter. Don't do it anymore." (Amazing how much she was beginning to sound like her mother!)

A few weeks later, the Pep Girls sat on the arm of the sofa. They looked at me with impish smiles and asked me to play our unnamed—yet clearly banned—game.

Pops: "We can't play that game anymore."
Ellie: "Why not?" (This was the point where I wanted to remind her that *she* was the one who ratted me out.)
Pops: "Your Mommy said we aren't allowed to sit on the arm."
Ellie (with a haughty air): "But she's not here now."

Yeah.

There's a difference in being a Daddy (parent) and a Pops (grandparent). Where once I was supposed to be the source of discipline, I have turned into a partner in crime. Willingness no longer matters: I am clearly an accomplice in whatever shenanigans are to come.

And I wouldn't have it any other way.

So, what about you?
We Back Niners have likely found ourselves both as coaches and mentors to our children, grandchildren, nephews, nieces—and even those kids that we coached in youth sports.

You probably don't need me to tell you the importance to the other person. Let's spend a minute talking about why it's important for *you*.

We may not see ourselves formally as mentors, but we are. The young people in our lives observe what we do. They will eventually choose to emulate it or reject it. For that reason, being cognizant of your role in this personal side of life is beneficial.

I wrote earlier that I've always learned something from mentoring. I never really considered myself as mentoring my daughters—I thought Barb and I were just "raising" them. In actuality, they were teaching me a lot about myself and life.

I will never forget when Kelli was about 17 years old and I told her the story of her mom and I dating in high school. I would leave Barb's house for the thirteen-minute drive home. She would gently ask me to call her when I got home, so she knew I made it safe (that's right, no cell phones, no texts back in those days).

I started doing that, but found we'd end up on the phone for another 45 minutes when I was ready to go to bed. So, I came up with an ingenious idea. I would call their phone (there were six kids, so her parents got them their own phone line) and let it ring once. That would be the alert that I was safely home. Smart, right?

With a hint of indignation on her face and the dismissive tone of a teen, Kelli retorted, *"Wow. You're like Mr. Insensitivity."*

Mindy and Kelli taught me empathy. I learned patience. I was forced to sharpen my skills in resilience. I learned to be nimbler. I became more present. And they showed me how to expand my views by challenging my own pre-conceived notions. I became more well-rounded as a human.

And yes, I learned sensitivity for the feelings of others.

The Practice Range:

It doesn't need to be formal ...

You are a mentor to someone—whether in business or your personal life. You have something of value to offer from your experiences and expertise. You may not want to be a role model, but you had at least one or two in your life.

Mentoring others to be the best they can be comes back full circle to us. Why not embrace it?

Here's an idea for you.

Identify one person in your business life and one in your personal circles that you can help. Don't ask if you can mentor them, simply do it. Be subtle and never pushy. Find ways to share your stories and provide a takeaway message. See what happens.

Captain Jack on the Green

There's this new Jack Russell Terrier (JRT) next door. His name is Otto. He's a young guy, like I once was. He's got that JRT air of superiority about him. Not cocky—just confident. I think he's a keeper.

He still has a lot to learn. We get a chance to say hello and to sniff each other, then I share my deep wisdom with him. I don't know if he's getting it or not, but I figure maybe a little of my smarts will enter his brain.

You gotta help the next gen of dogs. Otherwise, they can go sniffing around where it's dangerous or run out in front of a car. I've been there and done that. And I'm writing the book.

I figure the best thing I can help him with is his style. He's already mimicking my cavalier air while he walks. He's even trying the one flap up, one flap down look that I've made famous.

Makes me feel good. Makes him better.

Captain Jack out ...

The 17th Hole: Resilience

The Story of Dennis Walters

Golf is the great microcosm of life. You can hit a terrible shot and bounce off a tree back into the fairway. Or you can hit a great shot and land in a divot.

S**t happens to good people.

Dennis Walters was a rising star in the golf world. At 24 years old in 1974, he had traveled the world playing the game and was on the cusp of being thought of as one of the best players.

Then a golf cart accident left him paralyzed from the waist down.

At a hospital in Morristown, NJ, Dennis was told he would never walk again. And he hasn't. He was also told he'd never play golf again. And they were wrong.

With the help of his father and friends, Dennis began hitting golf balls from his wheelchair. That was good, but he couldn't take a wheelchair on the golf course, so they concocted a swivel chair mounted to a golf cart.

This invention allowed Dennis to do what no one before had done and what was considered impossible. He was playing golf without use of his legs!

Dennis went on to hone his game based on his physical disability. Through the help of people like Jack Nicklaus and Gary Player, he was able to finance clinics and trick shot events, which turned into *The Dennis Walters Golf Show.*

Since 1977, Dennis has traveled over 3.5 million miles and inspired audiences at over 3,000 performances. He's appeared in all fifty states, Mexico, Canada, and the United Kingdom. In 2019, he achieved golf's highest honor by being inducted into The World Golf Hall of Fame.

To learn more about Dennis Walters, visit his website at: https://www.denniswalters.com/

Adversity

Life is a complicated game to play. I think it boils down to answering the question of just how much disappointment you can endure and still carry on.

In the *Golf Films* documentary, Dennis Walters shared his recuperation story. He admitted that if he had known how to accomplish it, he would have committed suicide. He spoke of dark days and loads of doubt. Ultimately, as his story bears out, he lived an amazing life where he has shown millions of people—especially those with physical disabilities—that they can continue their lives doing the things they love. Like playing golf.

None of us are exempt from adversity. Just like every hole on a golf course includes obstacles to make it harder—sand traps, water, and out of bounds—each day we are presented with adversity.

A consequence of that is disappointment. Disappointment becomes manifest in many ways:

- Rejection
- Failure
- Loss of a loved one
- Financial hardship
- Relationship troubles
- Injury
- Accidents
- Health problems
- Worry about loved ones

This is a short list of a long number of reasons we can be disappointed. Depending on the strength and duration of that disappointment, the ramifications are severe and sometimes fatal—depression, anxiety, lost confidence, and addiction.

So how do we deal with disappointment?

I believe we start by understanding and preparing for adversity.

We know it's coming. While hopefully we don't start our morning with dread (and I'm afraid there may be a lot of people who do), we simply can't ignore that at some point it will touch our lives. A simple exercise of being ready for the physical, mental, and emotional challenges of adversity will help us cope with it better.

The Resilience Blueprint

My personal definition of resilience is being able to focus on moving forward no matter how bad a situation appears to be. It means being mentally tough.

I acknowledge that everyone will have their own definition of mental toughness. Since it's my book, let me give you mine.

Mental toughness is the ability to block out the noise, the distraction, and the fear to focus on the task at hand.

That noise may be external, but most often seems to be generated from within ourselves. The task at hand could be as simple as an unexpected schedule change, or it can be as significant as dealing with the death of a loved one.

We all have varying degrees of mental toughness. Those degrees could be based on if the task at hand is physical, emotional, or mental. They are certainly affected by importance and priority. And our own personal experiences and history will play a part in that noise in our heads.

The blueprint to resilience begins with mental toughness. Just like any muscle, we can strengthen this. And strengthening it should be a daily discipline.

Step 1: Identify when the noise comes and determine if it's external or internal.

If it's outside noise, figure out if the source is legitimate.

I only accept unsolicited advice from my most trusted advisors, and that's a small circle of people. They know who they are. Most people who give you advice or criticism are doing it for themselves—not for your benefit.

The inside noise is either bad self-talk or a response to the fear something may happen. On the former, if you can't figure out how to be kinder to yourself on your own, go get help. There are professionals that can help with that. On the latter, it becomes an issue of positive thinking.

I heard a former baseball pitcher on a radio interview once explain that he always had the mindset that he would get out of a bases loaded, one-out jam with a ground ball hit sharply to an infielder to turn an inning ending double-play. He never gave in to the fear of failure.

I've tried to keep that image in my own mind. It only takes one good pitch.

Bottom line: From where is the pressure coming and how do you best silence it?

Step 2: Focus on one spot.

When I'm playing golf and find that I'm having some mechanical issues in my swing, I will re-focus and concentrate on one tiny dimple on the golf ball. Making that focal point so targeted will push out everything else that is extraneous.

What is the one thing on which you can be intentionally focused in a situation that's causing you stress? Find that focal point.

Step 3: Eliminate emotion.

Yeah, like that's easy.

That's where mental toughness really becomes hard, right? We are emotional creatures and many of the predicaments in which we find ourselves have an emotional response. Unfortunately, when we guide our decisions based mostly on emotion, we get into trouble.

Being able to focus on the solution is the key. Don't get caught up in the "what ifs". I can't tell you how many times I've asked myself on the back nine during a round, "what if I only had made those three putts (or a myriad of other things)."

We do the same thing in our business and in our personal life.

We can't get caught in the blame game. It doesn't matter who's at fault. The current situation needs solving and we can't go back in time. Affixing blame to anyone, including ourselves, is wasted energy.

Breathing and physical movement are my key factors for this area. I will invest time in focusing on my breathing. Four breaths at a rate of four seconds in and four seconds out. Be mindful of your heart and brain rate.

Then I get physical. That means exercise and movement to change the brain chemicals. It's amazing how much clearer I can be when taking the dogs for a walk or doing strength training. The physical activity engages your brain and can help you solve problems.

Step 4: Trust your swing.

Bet on yourself.

In late 2021, Rory McIlroy celebrated his 20th career PGA win.

Avid golfers aren't surprised, as he was considered one of the top ten players in the world, arguably even in the top five. McIlroy had won four major championships within those twenty wins—which makes him one of the great golfers of all time. However, he had hit a bit of a dry spell over the previous couple of years. This was surprising to everyone who follows the game, including his peers, because of his immense talent.

Rory admitted after the victory that over his dry spell he was trying too hard to be someone else. As many golfers (especially amateurs) are wont to do, they tinker and overthink in an effort to emulate someone else. Rory is human and acknowledged that he did the same. He was wowed by some of his peers in a quest to hit the ball farther off the tee, although he was already considered one of the best in that category.

How ironic that many of us amateurs are trying very hard to be him!

McIlroy said that he finally realized that being Rory McIlroy was good enough. Instead of trying to be someone he wasn't, he committed to being his best self.

This doesn't occur just in golf.

We don't give ourselves enough credit for what we've accomplished and experienced. In golfing terms, we don't trust our swing. So instead, we try to be someone else.

I've been guilty of that. In my career as a consultant, I've at times tried too hard to mirror mentors and coaches. Instead of following their examples, I tried to be them. It doesn't work. Being Dan Weedin is good enough.

What about you?

Have you caught yourself trying too hard to be more like someone else—to the point that you forgot that your talent is already exceptional? Do you give yourself credit for your accomplishments and experiences? Do you trust your swing always?

To unleash your maximum potential, you must be all in on yourself. If you're going to bet your career and life on someone, shouldn't it be you?

The next time you start doubting your own abilities or find yourself changing your "swing" to try to look more like someone else you admire, look in the mirror and simply remind yourself that you and your game are more than good enough.

The Practice Range:

Resilience is a blend of mental toughness, grit, perseverance, determination, and confidence. Then you must add the all-important ability to focus. If it were easy, we'd all be doing it constantly.

This is one area I highly encourage you to commit to practicing. Make resilience a daily discipline.

I suggest you consider working on mindfulness exercises to incorporate breathing and focus. If you're struggling with doing it on your own, find someone to help you. Ask your most trusted advisors to hold you accountable—especially those who know you best, like family, close friends, and business colleagues. Make sure you create metrics to measure success.

Finally, develop a game plan that you follow every day. Whatever you invest in improving your personal resilience will come back to you many times over. It's your ultimate ROI.

Captain Jack on the Green

I once had an infected tooth. Dan saw it, but I felt it first.

He thought it was some dirt under my eye. When he went to rub it away, he realized it was a hole.

That's right. A hole.

I guess I had what Dr. Craig (my doctor) calls an abscessed tooth. It caused an infection that went up through my cheek and busted through on the other side.

When Dan heard this, he was stunned. He told Dr. Craig that I hadn't been acting any differently. That I had shown no signs of being hurt.

Dr. Craig told him what I already knew. JRTs—we are tough sons of bitches (and I mean that literally, not in your colloquial way). He said that we can handle a pain that would put you humans crying in a fetal position on the floor. Well, he didn't put it that way, but that's how I inferred it.

Not long after, Dr. Craig did his thing and fixed my face without making me look less handsome. He's the best. Bella doesn't like him too much because he's extracted all her teeth. She seems to be holding a grudge. Me? I think he's pretty cool, even if he did go to a college with a cat as a mascot.

I think this is what Dan calls resilience. I call it nothing. It's dealing with stuff that happens to us without letting it get us down. I guess you can say we dogs are adaptable. We make things work, no matter what.

Even when we have a hole in our head.

Captain Jack out ...

In the previous chapter, I shared a lot of thoughts about resilience and dealing with disappointment, but I didn't mention one area that may have the potential of being the deepest greenside bunker.

Relationships are challenging, to say the least. We humans have varied ways to communicate our thoughts and feelings. We are all "wired" in different ways. We have histories and experiences that mold our worldview. And, we have learned behaviors and attitudes from observing others in our family and associations.

Even the best relationships are fragile.

I've been beyond blessed to have found my life partner back in high school in 1982. Barb and I were married in 1986, despite my faux pax on the wedding invitations!

We've had a great life, but it's not been without challenges. You can't be together for forty years and be on the same page all the time. But to Barb's point referenced earlier, we've always been in the same book!

I'm also beyond lucky to have daughters who I consider to be "best friends". They have wonderful partners who we think the world of. Not everybody gets that, so Barb and I cherish this.

These relationships were founded and developed even with the inevitable parent-child experiences, where tipping points can go in any direction.

The deepest pain can be caused by family relationships that have been strained or completely lost. While friends and associations can be transitioned, family can't. I can attest that in my own life some of this strife remains and may not ever be resolved. You might have that, too.

As we walk the Back Nine journey, it becomes ever more important to identify the relationships that you want to nurture, those that you want to distance, and those that fall somewhere in between.

There are four different categories of relationships that should be weighted differently, in my opinion. The first and most portentous is the one with your spouse or significant other. The next most consequential is with your children and grandchildren. The third is with your siblings (including those acquired through marriage). Finally, comes your extended family.

There is a time where who's to blame or at fault no longer matters. It comes down to how much energy you want to invest. I'm a believer in fighting for relationships—especially in the order of categories mentioned. Being resilient requires that you're fighting for the relationships you want the most.

The 18th Hole: Legacy

Why Don't You Hit It Then?

It was 1988. The place was Inglewood Country Club in Kenmore, WA (a suburb of Seattle). The GTE Classic was in town, and I had secured passes because my brother-in-law, who worked for GTE at the time, had a pass to give me. The GTE Classic was a stop in what was at the time called The Senior Tour for professional golfers 50 years old and up. Today it's called the Champions Tour.

I was standing behind the ropes on the first hole watching a legend tee off. Arnold Palmer was known to the golfing world as "The King." His influence went well beyond golf. His name was known worldwide by golfers, businesspeople, titans of industry—and really anyone who was paying attention to life. Even someone with no golfing background knew the name Arnold Palmer (even if simply ordering the lemonade and iced tea drink named after him).

In 1988, Arnie (as his legion of fans known as Arnie's Army called him) was about 58 years old. I was just 23, so that seemed ancient to me. Funny, that I'm just about to that age as I write this book.

I'd not watched Arnie in his prime, but as an avid golfer knew him as the iconic figure of the game. He had a charisma and personality that was magnetic. I made the decision that on this day, I would bypass all the other big names playing and follow Arnold Palmer for all eighteen holes. As I look back, it's one of my sports highlights.

One scene is vivid in my memory.

On one Par 4-hole, Arnie had hit left of the fairway and found his ball stymied behind a tree. I was behind him in the gallery to his left, waiting eagerly as everyone else to watch one of the greatest get out of this predicament.

He paused and very studiously surveyed the situation. Suddenly, a woman's voice broke through the silence.

"But Arnie, I saw you hit this shot in one of your golf videos ..."

Mr. Palmer turned in her direction off my left shoulder. You could hear a tee drop. He then reached out his club as if to hand it to her, and said, *"Okay ... why don't you hit it for me then?"*

And he smiled.

The gallery erupted in laughter. He took a few more seconds and then hit a marvelous shot on the green bypassing the tree that had likely infuriated amateurs like me.

Arnie was famous for the admiration of his fans. It was that charm and warmth that helped fuel the evangelical following.

But that charm is only part of the legacy he left behind. It is universally believed by people in professional golf that Arnold Palmer is responsible for the large purses they play for on the PGA Tour. While he wasn't always the very best player, he had the biggest group of fans and the television audience loved him. At a time when televising golf was incredibly difficult, people tuned in to watch their expressive hero.

Arnold Palmer was the guiding force in what's now the Champions Tour. Shortly after turning 50 years old in 1980, Arnie went on to play on the tour and provide both the credibility and sponsor needed to take a fledgling idea and turn it into a business. Now, professionals over 50 had a place to go and still compete and earn money. Today, the Champions Tour still ranks as one of the top three sponsored tours in the world.

On top of that, Arnold Palmer founded The Golf Channel, became a golf course designer, and created Arnold Palmer International, an organization that builds hospitals and airports while funding philanthropic ventures around the world. Chip in a line of clothing, a beverage distribution company that sells cans of *Arnold Palmer* drinks, and countless other business ventures— and you have a brand name and influence that will last for generations.

Arnold Palmer created a legacy in golf, business, aviation, clothing, philanthropy, medicine, and food that has outlived him and will remain vibrant forever.

Spanning the Generations

It's easy to say, *"Well, people like Arnold Palmer can create a legacy, but I'm just a regular person."*

Arnold Palmer wasn't born into fame and fortune. He was just a "regular" guy hailing from Latrobe, PA, a rural farming community near Pittsburgh. His family was not well off, and he had to work and struggle for everything that he achieved as a golfer and businessperson.

I've got to believe that if you're reading this book, creating some sort of legacy is important for you. Of the myriad of potential legacy options, I'd like to focus on what I consider to be the top three: family, business, and philanthropy.

Family:

We should all have some biological literacy. That's a term I heard used, and sadly I wasn't literate enough to remember to whom the credit goes.

Honor those not alive yet, as we are their ancestors.

When I heard this phrase, it caused me to pause. As a history major and the son of a serial genealogist, the term *ancestors* was forged in my brain. Ancestors were those people who lived a long time ago and were basically all deceased. They weren't me.

But now I realize that I am going to be someone's ancestor. As a grandfather, I am now the third generation for someone. That acknowledgement took my limited concept of legacy to a new place.

But my lineage won't end there. I'm the descendant of people who at one time were my age and perhaps not thinking past their own living family members. Yet here I am—and my grandchildren are the future.

I used to think that legacy was primarily a financial gift. If someone was wealthy enough, they could create generational wealth for a long line of family members who may never meet them. Arnold Palmer created generational wealth for his family. However, there is much more than financial when it comes to family.

Consider what legacy you can leave in these areas:

- Wisdom
- Education
- Culture

- Music
- Language
- Arts
- Sports
- Generosity
- Kindness
- Faith and Spirituality

As I observe Barb teaching our granddaughters to cook and bake, I can imagine them keeping those memories for the rest of their lives, and maybe even passing the same thing on to their children and grandchildren.

THAT is legacy.

Business:
Do you own a business? What do you want that business to look like once you've left?

Everyone exits their business—either vertically or horizontally. What's your wish for what you've built and the people you've employed?

All too often, it's easy to get caught up in today's financial statements, spreadsheets, and reports. If you own a business, think about strategy for the future. It might involve your family. It will definitely involve your employees.

Many of my best clients invested time and resources into these questions well before their time to leave was at hand. Those who do so are creating a generational business for their family, employees, customers, and community.

Philanthropy:

Think of the story of Arnold Palmer. One of his greatest legacies comes in the twenty-nine hospitals scattered throughout the United States treating women and children in five different specialties. How many people are alive today because of Arnold Palmer's acumen in golf, business, and philanthropy?

As a proud Rotarian since November 1993, I'm hoping that the time, talent, and treasure shared through this great organization have impacted people around the world by providing polio vaccinations, clean water, food, shelter, and hope.

Many of you reading this will have charities and causes that are near and dear to your heart. You may have already made plans to fund these organizations after your death. If you haven't, here is an opportunity to be a legacy for those who might never know you existed.

So, what about you?

Have you invested time in considering what you want your legacy to be?

We all will have a legacy—whether we desire one or not. Spending time on this earth interacting with other humans and the planet makes that as certain as death and taxes.

We should all want to take control of our legacy, as opposed to letting others try to figure it out.

Just like you take time to create a vision for your lifestyle finances, relationships, and business, invest a little time on what you want to influence for the future.

The Practice Range:

Planning.

We all talk about plans, but planning is the action that spawns those plans.

This is where the divot is created in the ground. Build a foundation for the future by taking each of the categories—family, business, and philanthropy—and create a game plan.

This plan should involve your Will (you do have one, right?), investments, passions, family, friends, associations, and employees/co-workers.

Gather your most trusted advisors and have them help you start a legacy plan. You can always make changes, but you can't if you don't have a plan to start.

Captain Jack on the Green

We dogs have a legacy.

It's not money—that's what humans focus on too much.

It's not fame or power.

It's our spirit.

Look, if you've ever owned a pet (and, of course, I'm partial to dogs), you remember everything about them after they are gone. You remember how they played with you, slept on the bed next to you, and all the shenanigans they got into.

You can see their face right now, can't you?

That's legacy.

Captain Jack out ...

Eating Ice Cream

"More!"

It was March 17, 2011. I was standing in my parents' two-bedroom assisted living apartment. The hospice people had just left after speaking with Dad. In the room with me were Mom, Barb, my sister Rita, and my daughter Mindy, who happened to be home from university for spring break.

Dad knew what hospice meant. Shortly after they left, he slipped into unconsciousness. We called them back, and they confirmed the dying process was underway and it wouldn't be long.

I had come to understand that people in a comatose state can still hear and comprehend. Each of us took a turn talking to Dad and I could see on his face that he heard us. After everyone said something, I came up with an idea to allow others to do the same.

In order, I called my Aunt Gloria, brother Les, sister Kathy, and daughter Kelli. They were all living in various places around the country at the time. We had purchased a ticket for Kelli to fly home, but it was for the next day and it would likely be too late for her to speak to him.

I put the phone on speaker mode and up to Dad's ear. Each person spoke their goodbyes and, again, I felt that Dad heard every word—even though he couldn't verbally respond.

After Kelli was done, a huge pall fell over the air. As luck would have it—maybe thanks to St. Patrick on his feast day—a young staffer named Sarah came in with chocolate chip mint ice cream and asked if we would like some. I told her that was exactly what we needed.

As I was enjoying my ice cream, a scoop fell on the floor right below my foot without me knowing it.

Suddenly, all of the women in the room literally screamed at me in unison, *"STOP!"*

It was as if I was a helicopter in a no-fly zone over the White House! *"What???"* I exclaimed.

I was informed of the ice cream under my foot and the dire implications if I stepped on it.

Really?

We all broke out in much-needed laughter.

Barb was seated next to Dad holding his hand, keeping him part of the group. She said to him, "Your *son. He almost stepped on ice cream!*"

Like Lazarus coming out of the tomb, Dad sat bolt upright in his recliner, stared straight at Barb and exclaimed, *"Did someone say ice cream?"*

We were stunned. I said, *"Yeah, Dad. We're all eating ice cream. Do you want some?"*

He turned to me with a wild-eyed look and exclaimed, *"Certainly!"*

I left the room and passed the hospice workers on the way to the kitchen. I told them what happened, and they were astonished. Sarah said she would bring the ice cream for Dad.

Back in the room, we all watched as Dad devoured the ice cream Barb fed him. Sarah stuck around to watch, as she was very fond of Dad. As Barb shoveled his favorite food into his mouth, she asked him a question that would normally be reserved for a 3-year-old. *"Now Dad, wasn't that nice of Sarah to bring you ice cream? What do you say to her?"*

Dad turned to Sarah with the same mad look in his eyes, gulped the ice cream and blurted out with earnestness …

"MORE!"

His last words could not be more fitting.

More

More.

Dad wanted more ice cream, and we wanted more time with him.

In reminiscence, that one word is a statement for all of us to consider—whether we are playing the Front or Back Nine of life. Shouldn't we be asking for MORE right now? Finding ways to create MORE right now? Being MORE fearless, MORE forgiving, MORE present?

I surmise that at the end of our lives, we will still desire MORE— no matter what we've accomplished. However, it's a reminder that we are here now and, with good fortune, we still have a whole lot MORE time now.

So, let's do something with it.

Doing MORE Now

It's taken me over forty years of playing golf to embrace being in the moment.

It's not easy to focus on only the next shot. My mind can get distracted on the last hole that I three-putt, or the scary shot over the water on the next hole that I haven't even gotten to yet.

The very best golfers in the world have found a way to focus on just the next shot. As a basketball coach, I used to preach to my players to focus on the next play. And all of us in our careers have found ways to become present at the most important times.

However, do we all do that *enough*?

The 19th Hole is widely known as the place golfers celebrate after the round with food and libation. It's that special place to gloat in victory and make excuses for poor play. To laugh, to enjoy, and to keep the round going a little longer.

While that period of celebration will end with everyone dispersing back home, our Back Nine celebration can be continuous if only we allow it to be.

As we close out this book, here is a closing Par 4 idea to help you live MORE in both your business and life pursuits:

The Drive: There's a lot of moving parts to a golf swing. If you have too many "swing thoughts" you end up complicating things and the results are not very good.

While my swing thought for a round will often change based on how I'm playing, the one constant is my head. As in most sports, if your head stays steady, the rest of the swing has a better chance of being good.

Keep your head steady.

It's easy to get into our own head with what I call "stinking thinking". How we talk to ourselves is critical in business and in our personal life. While self-deprecation works in humor, it's not so good when we mean it.

Be good to yourself. The MORE you are, the MORE you will get in return.

The Approach: Jin Young Ko is one of the top women professional golfers in the world. As I write this, she is ranked #1. In her last tournament, she finished by hitting the green in regulation sixty-three straight times. If you're a golfer, the enormity of that is unfathomable. For reference, Tiger Woods' record for consecutive greens hit in regulation is twenty-nine. I think mine is three.

Hitting the green in regulation means that you've reached the green in the number of strokes to allow two putts for par. On a Par 4, that means two strokes. Jin Young Ko is the best in the world because she puts herself in a position to make par more often than most.

Put yourself in good position MORE in your business and your life.

You accomplish this by being strategic about risk and reward—that fine balance of fearlessness and practicality. You accomplish this by staying positive, being open to new ideas, seeking advice from experts, and trusting your gut.

There's no doubt we will occasionally make mistakes. But the more consistent we are, the more birdie putts we will be attempting and that makes life more fun.

The Lag Putt: Professional golfers expect to make their first putts more often than not. For me, I really just want a stress-free second putt! On longer putts, I want to get to a distance where my playing partner says, "That's good." On shorter putts, I will be bolder. Regardless of length, if I'm thinking of something else, then my effort will likely lead to a missed putt and a more stressful next one. I need to be fully present.

To experience MORE, we need to invest in being present. Really present. That means more than being physically there. And I admit, this is hard for me. It's become a discipline that I must practice and be intentional.

We all get busy, and our brains are so complex that we can have a gazillion thoughts processing all at the same time.

When I recognize that in myself, I literally stop what I'm doing and focus on my breathing in an effort to slow my heart and brain rate. I then internally whisper to myself, *"One thing at a time."*

That might mean re-focusing on the Pep Girls when we're together. It might mean re-focusing on writing the next chapter of my book, speaking at an event, or being in discussion with a client. Heck, it might simply mean being present with Barb as we are watching a movie at home together.

Being present is a skill. It demands practice and discipline. It also requires patience because we all will fail at times. Yet if you master this, you will get MORE.

The Tap In: One thing I've learned is that to score better, you don't need more birdies, you need fewer double bogeys (or worse). That's why I work from tee to green to tap in for no worse than bogey.

There are few things I love hearing more than the sound of the ball hitting the bottom of the cup. I also like hearing one of my Jumanji pals saying, *"That's good ... pick it up."*

When we can focus on keeping our head in the game, simplifying life, putting ourselves in good positions for success, and staying present, we ultimately will achieve so much MORE in life than we imagined.

We will truly be unleashed as we continue our Back Nine Walking.

Captain Jack on the Green

Celebrate.

That's my advice.

I don't know how many more walks around the block I will get. I'm almost 15 years old and even by Jack Russell standards, that's getting up there. But I don't care.

I celebrate every day. Why? Because every day and every moment is different. We dogs can literally smell it.

I live a good life. I'm loved by my family and return that love. I also now have new family - Ellie and Maddie are just like I was when I was a puppy. They bring me energy and unconditional love. I love them.

I only am concerned with the now—not yesterday or tomorrow. I eat the best food and get my exercise. I'm happy.

Dan and I hope the same for you. Go be happy. Get MORE out of your walks around the neighborhood. And go be UNLEASHED.

There's no better way to live.

Captain Jack out ...

About the Author

Dan Weedin is an experienced entrepreneur, thought leader, author, and award-winning speaker who has a passion for consulting, advising, and mentoring other entrepreneurs and business professionals.

He has the rare ability to translate his success in the insurance industry, public speaking, non-profit world, and athletic coaching into applicable and transferable principles that dramatically improve the effectiveness of those business owners and executives with whom he works.

Dan's educational background includes formal education, certifications, and ongoing professional development. He is a 1987 graduate of the University of Washington where he received his Bachelor of Arts degree in History.

In 2010, Dan was accredited as a Master Mentor by internationally renowned consultant and mentor Alan Weiss. He is one of fewer than 50 people in the world holding this exclusive accreditation. In 2012, Dan was inducted into the Million Dollar Consultant™ Hall of Fame.

Dan is an active member of his community. He is a past president of his Rotary Club and has served as an elected official for a public school board of directors, including as board president. Among the numerous community organizations with which he has been involved include the Sons of the American Revolution, Olympic College Foundation, Kathleen Sutton Fund, Toastmasters International, and his church.

On crisp, Fall Friday nights, you will find Dan in the press box at North Kitsap High School, where he has served as the "Voice of the Vikings", as the stadium announcer for the high school football team since 2003. He enjoys playing golf, cooking, drinking bourbon, listening to all kinds of books and podcasts, and being walked by his two faithful canine companions, Captain Jack and Bella.

Dan married Barb, his high school sweetheart, in 1986. They have two adult daughters, Mindy and Kelli, and Dan is now "Pops" to the two most perfect granddaughters ever. He and Barb reside in Poulsbo, WA, across the Puget Sound, just West of Seattle.

Made in the USA
Middletown, DE
22 July 2022